URBAN TRIBES

NATIVE AMERICANS IN THE CITY

Edited by Lisa Charleyboy and Mary Beth Leatherdale

annick press
Toronto • New York • Vancouver

Page 135 constitutes an extension of this copyright page.
Cover collage and handlettering by Inti Amaterasu. Graffiti artwork by Steven Paul Judd.
Interior Design by Inti Amaterasu

Annick Press Ltd.

We acknowledge the support of the Access Copyright Foundation, the Canada Council for the Arts, the Ontario Arts Council, and the Government of Canada through the Canada Book Fund (CBF) for our publishing activities.

Cataloging in Publication
  Urban lives : Native Americans in the city / edited by Lisa Charleyboy and Mary Beth Leatherdale.
Issued in print and electronic formats.
ISBN 978-1-55451-751-0 (bound).--ISBN 978-1-55451-750-3 (pbk.).--
ISBN 978-1-55451-752-7 (html).--ISBN 978-1-55451-753-4 (pdf)

        1. Native peoples--Urban residence--Canada--Juvenile literature.
2. Indians of North America--Urban residence--United States--Juvenile
literature. 3. Native youth--Canada--Social conditions--Juvenile
literature. 4. Indian youth--United States--Social conditions--Juvenile
literature. 5. Native youth--Canada--Biography--Juvenile literature.
6. Indian youth--United States--Biography--Juvenile literature.
I. Charleyboy, Lisa, editor II. Leatherdale, Mary Beth, editor

E98.U72U73 2015   j305.897'071   C2015-900848-4
                                               C2015-900849-2
Published in the U.S.A. by Annick Press (U.S.) Ltd.

Printed in Canada

Visit us at: www.annickpress.com
Visit us at:urbannativetribes.com
Visit Lisa Charleyboy at: www.lisacharleyboy.com
Visit Mary Beth Leatherdale at: marybethleatherdale.com

Also available in e-book format. Please visit www.annickpress.com/ebooks.html for more details. Or scan

To Jarret, who's ignited many conversations that fueled
my desire to create this space – LC

For Jeff, with thanks for being on my team – MBL

**Two-eyed seeing "recognizes the benefits of seeing
from one eye with the strengths of Indigenous ways
of knowing, from the other eye the strengths of the
Western ways of knowing, and using both of these
eyes together to create new forms of understanding
and insight."**

*– Elder Albert Marshall
(Mi'kmaq, Eskasoni First Nation)*

Contents

In each City Quote, the traditional territory the city is on is acknowledged. Traditional territory is the geographic area that a First Nation or Native Tribe traditionally used for hunting, trapping, fishing, gathering plants, and obtaining water. It's also where ceremonies and economic and cultural activities took place.

"Living in the city, I was the only brown kid, never mind the only Native kid, on the hockey team or in the classroom. That was difficult. My parents did encourage me from a young age to bring my traditional regalia into school and put on a demonstration and try and teach my classmates a bit about the culture. I was given the background to share that and help educate people. What it did for me on a personal level was it reaffirmed the fact that my culture was important for my personal identity."

—Wab Kinew (Anishinaabe, Onigaming First Nation) lives in Winnipeg. He is the Associate Vice-President for Indigenous Relations at the University of Winnipeg and correspondent with Aljazeera America.

Roots

When I was sixteen, I officially became a punk rocker. I know you're probably asking yourself, "How does someone 'officially' become a punk rocker?" More probably you're asking yourself, "Why would someone want to officially become a punk rocker?" For me, becoming a punk rocker was a simple physical action but a very difficult emotional and intellectual one. The physical part is that I got my sister to take a pair of scissors and then a razor and cut, shave, and shape my hair into a really big Mohawk.

This isn't such a big deal today but back in 1981 it kind of was. The rebellious punk movement was still defining itself, having moved beyond the chaotic Sex Pistols era of the 1970s and into a more focused and super-charged political and social movement. To wear your hair in a Mohawk back then meant that you wanted to make a big statement. But you were also prepared to be teased and taunted by your peers, picked on by many of your teachers, treated as an embarrassment by your own family, and certainly singled out by the cops every chance they got.

So why bother, right? Why purposely choose to become the focus of abuse and disdain and laughter? Why walk around looking different than your peers, so many of whom you don't feel a connection with? Why choose to stand out from this crowd that you feel is so conservative, so mild, so accepting of everything, this crowd of young people who seem afraid–afraid of exploring their world, of making comments about it, of speaking out against what they clearly see is wrong? Why separate yourself from a herd like that?

Let me back up a minute. At the age of 16, I'd just experienced a very difficult time in my life. I was trying to come to terms with the realization I wasn't perfect, that I was actually facing an illness, but one I didn't know how to beat. It wasn't a physical illness. I had just quit as the captain of my football team not because I couldn't physically play but because mentally I had no drive anymore. A year before I'd begun to give up on life and had been feeling it drain from me every day until on the night of my sixteenth birthday, I couldn't take it anymore and tried to drain all of it out at once. My attempt at taking my own life that night thankfully failed. I am so grateful today as a person who can look back a little ways and see how great the path that we call every day life actually is. But this isn't just a story about that. This little story I'm trying to tell you before you jump into the pages of this amazing book that is *Urban Tribes* is actually about finding my roots.

That word roots strikes me as kind of interesting at this moment. By cutting my hair into a Mohawk, by cutting most of it off on the sides of my head right down to my roots, I was actually on the road to finding my true roots.

What made my Mohawk particularly abrasive to my teachers is that, at the time I cut it this way, I was being forced to attend an all-boys Jesuit high school called Brebeuf. Jean de Brébeuf was a real life person, a man who came to Canada in the mid 1600s to bring Christianity to the First Nations of Quebec and Ontario. Long story short, the same Jesuits who ran my high school held their namesake in great regard, and every student who came through the doors of Brebeuf was reminded almost daily that the savages who ended up capturing him and then torturing him to death were the Mohawks, the same ones who wore their hair down the middle of their heads. I'll never forget the first day I walked through the doors of this school I so desperately wanted to get kicked out of, and seeing the looks on the Jesuits' faces as I walked proudly by, my hairstyle, I hoped, sending fear into their very hearts. My haircut became something even more symbolic than a contemporary statement. It was a historical one as well. With a simple haircut, I began the long road to finding my own roots.

I come from a mixed blood family of mostly Irish, Scottish, and Anishinaabe (Ojibwe) heritage. What I only now realize I was doing back in my rebellious teen years was rebelling not just from my anger at a system that seemed loaded to only help those who held all the power already, but rebelling against the idea that it was only cool to try and force yourself into being a certain type. At my school at the time, it was only cool to be the preppy one with the right haircut and all the right clothes. If you did this, then all the right friends would naturally flock to you. I realized I didn't fit into that mold. The rest of my life to date is coming to the realization that molds might not be the best thing for us humans to try to fit ourselves into. We're not jello, after all.

I no longer wear my hair in a Mohawk. That particular style lasted about three or four years before I decided it was time to move on. But what that original act of rebellion did do was set me on a path that I still walk today. My life to date has been one of questioning things that don't always seem to add up. As a mixed-blood person, I can't believe or accept that my First Nations ancestors were savages and that my European ancestors came to North America to teach these savages the true path. I refuse to let others tell me who I should be. I refuse to try and be somebody or something that I am not in order to fit into the crowd. And I especially refuse to allow those who have all the power to treat those who don't with impunity. As a person who has the blood of both the European and the First Nations in me, that day I cut my hair into the style of those who were being oppressed was the day I accepted that, in a lot of ways, I was no longer part of the "in" crowd.

It's weird to think about but a simple haircut can really do that. It can really change not just others' views of you but your view of yourself and the world around you. Come to think of it, maybe it isn't that weird after all. How we physically present ourselves to the world is how we want the world to understand us, how we want the world to read us, so to speak. And being a writer, I want the world to read me carefully. It's my hope, dear reader, that the world reads you exactly the way you want it to, as well.

– Joseph Boyden

Editors' Notes

"So, just how connected are you to your Indigenous roots if you live downtown?"

It happened at a gathering last year when I was asked this very question. I found myself blundering a bit as I was trying to come up with some concrete examples so I could prove to this Irish man just how Indian I am. Would my community involvement do it? Or how about my strong Tsilhqot'in lineage? Suddenly I realized how absurd this situation was. Why was I feeling the need to prove myself?

I shouldn't have been so surprised by his question. I and many other urban Indigenous youth have grown up being told that we can't really be Native if we are living a "modern" life in the city. There's this deeply held notion that in order to be authentically Indigenous, one must live on a reservation, or one's traditional territory, and have a deep connection to one's land.

Yet for hundreds of years, Natives have chosen to make their homes in cities for educational and employment opportunities. Others migrated to metropolitan areas because they were forced off their "rez" due to government policies, or residential schools, or because they were taken into foster care.

Fifty-six percent of Natives live in urban settings both in United States and Canada. (see p.130)

Indigenous, urban, and "millennial." We are the focus of many studies, reports, and speeches and are mentioned often in mainstream media. And yet we are still somehow intangible for many. And in some cosmopolitan cities, we are almost rendered invisible.

We're diverse in our opinions, lived experiences, and points of cultural connection but similar in our desire for defining our identity and creating culturally safe spaces in our communities and our cities.

– Lisa Charleyboy (Tsilhqot'in from Tsi Del Del)

In *Urban Tribes*, we wanted to shine a light on the underreported stories of urban Natives – the artists and the academics, the bankers and the biologists – the growing number of urban Native professionals who are still largely invisible.

I grew up in a rural community in southwestern Ontario going to school with Native kids from the Delaware Nation at Moraviantown. But in my adult life in Toronto, the tens of thousands of Natives who I shared the city with were largely invisible to me. And, urban Native youth were rarely – if ever – discussed in terms of an audience for the children's books and magazines I was working on.

In 2012, the Idle No More movement really woke me up to the fact that what I, my family, and many of my friends and colleagues "knew" about the urban Native experience was based almost entirely on tragic news reports and the underlying stereotypes and prejudices they often inadvertently fuel. And I wanted to be part of changing that.

Our research and interviews for *Urban Tribes* were driven by our curiosity to learn more about the wide-ranging experiences of urban Native youth and the ways in which they stay connected to culture. We reached out to young people from ages 13 to 35 living in large cities across North America and asked them to share their stories in their way through their words, music, and visual art. Their opinions and experiences are diverse, but the racism and discrimination they face is often disheartening. Yet these youth share a common perspective on their culture. Whether they are living in New York City or Vancouver, Los Angeles or Winnipeg, whether they've just moved to the city or their family has lived there for generations, Native culture and community are an essential and cherished part of their urban lives, an integral part of their identity, and a key component of their successes. We're honored to share the words and works of these Indigenous youth. They inspired us and we hope they inspire you.

– *Mary Beth Leatherdale*

TRIBAL CITIZENS

Native millennials stay connected
to and draw strength from their culture
and identity in diverse ways in the city.

Rooted in Culture

An interview with Tyson Atleo

Tyson *?ikaatius Atleo is the next in line to fill a twenty-seventh-generation Hereditary Chief's seat of the Ahousaht First Nation of the Nuu-chah-nulth people from the west coast of British Columbia. He shares how he connects to his cultural values living in Vancouver.

Where did you grow up?
People always ask me, "Were you raised on reserve?" Sometimes out of curiosity, but I would argue mostly as a way to measure "how Indian I am." As if being raised on reserve makes you more First Nations than someone raised off reserve. The reality is that I was actually born in downtown Vancouver. I went to elementary school and early high school in a north Surrey neighborhood, before moving to Nanaimo to finish high school. What people have a hard time understanding, especially non-Native people, is that I also consider myself to have been raised in Ahousaht, my reserve. I've been traveling to and from the reserve since I was born. Ahousaht is a place from where much of my cultural education and identity comes from.

Why do you live in the city?
I am drawn to living in the city for a number of reasons— most notably a combination of employment opportunities and lifestyle. Unfortunately, there are not a lot of diverse employment opportunities on reserve. Also, I am attracted to certain aspects of lifestyle in the city. The diversity of cultures and unique opportunities in the city, such as organized sports, good cuisine, and meeting like-minded people are attractive offers. But I do get away from the city quite often to reconnect with nature, my culture, and for leisure as a way to keep my life in balance.

Do you feel pressure living in Vancouver to get caught up in the consumerist culture?
Absolutely. The media not only bombards us with advertisements, but also in order to be accepted into most city cultures, you must dress and act the part. You can have the most amazing ideas, a genuine personality, and intellectual superpowers, but if you do not look like you belong to the group with which you seek an audience, your message will likely fall on deaf ears.

What do you wish you could change about city life?
A great deal. The city really is representational of the elitist attitude our species exhibits toward the rest of the natural environment: that only humans matter, that we care not for what needs to be destroyed in order to maintain our desired level of comfort and convenience. City life will only change once our economic systems change. We must stop overconsuming.

Passionate about supporting the spiritual, social, and economic well-being of Indigenous peoples, Tyson Atleo has been raised as a leader to respect Nuu-chah-nulth cultural values.

"People always ask me, 'Were you raised on reserve?' Sometimes out of curiosity, but I would argue mostly as a way to measure 'how Indian I am.' As if being raised on reserve makes you more First Nations than someone raised off reserve."

How do you integrate Indigenous values in your day-to-day life in the city?

The four pillars of our Nuu-chah-nulth cultural values are love one another, teach one another, respect one another, and care for one another. Our values teach us how to "manage relationships" with all of creation—other people and the environment. All of our day-to-day decisions impact our lives and the lives of others. Be kind and courteous to others in everything that you do. Be mindful of what you purchase and of all your decisions and actions. Be conscious of what you put in your body. These are simple things that can mean a great difference in what can be a very cold and harsh world.

What do you do when you're feeling overwhelmed in the city? How do you connect to nature?

In any major city, nature is still not far away. We are fortunate in Vancouver to have access to a lot of great wilderness within an hour's drive. Committing to being active is key. Another key is to find beauty in all nature. I owe a lot to my dog. She gets me out of the house and to the park or to the hiking trail on a regular basis. One tree at the park is no less special than one tree in the middle of a rain forest. Whether you are watching birds on the seawall, a squirrel at the local park, or admiring the flowers in a garden, it is all precious.

HALIFAX

Traditional Territory - Mi'kmaq

"Living as an urban warrior in Halifax has strengthened my spirit culturally. I see many Natives feeling welcomed here by the Native community and being free and empowered to tap into our roots. The friendship center offers more than I had growing up on the rez. Halifax has embraced my #SpeakMikmaq language movement, encouraging me to strive higher."

– *Savannah "Savvy" Simon*
(Mi'kmaq, Elsipogtog First Nation), founder
#SpeakMikmaq, motivational speaker

Food with Thought
An appetite for ancestral diets

Before European colonization, Indigenous peoples across North America relied on hunting, fishing, and agriculture for their food. But government policy to try to assimilate Natives weakened the connection to traditional food practices. Within a few generations, their diet changed dramatically from traditional foods like buffalo, deer, salmon, wild rice, and berries to processed foods. And with that change in diet came an increase in diabetes, obesity, and respiratory and circulatory disease among Natives.

In large cities, more and more Natives are looking to the nutritional value of traditional foods and using the abundant food resources to follow an ancestral diet. While similar to the popular Paleo Diet, which encourages people to eat meat, fish, fruit, and vegetables and avoid dairy, refined sugar, and grains, the ancestral diet is more than another foodie trend.

Blogger Chantal Rondeau (Hanjek Hudan Clan, Little Salmon Carmacks First Nation) left her home in the small town of Carmacks, Yukon, when she was just 18 years old. Her journey took her from Edmonton to Calgary, Winnipeg to Whitehorse and to Vancouver, where she lives now. No matter where she might hang up her Lululemon hoodie, she stays connected to "home" through her food.

"No matter what urban city that I'm in, I have traditional foods in my house," says Rondeau. "It's the connection to my land. I have an apartment-size freezer full of moose meat and caribou meat. I have salmon from the Yukon and Alaska. I have frozen berries that I harvested up in the Yukon. I have canned salmon. My food will always keep me connected to my inner spirituality and my inner traditions because it feels like my land; these animals come from my land."

Thosh Collins (Pima) is a huge advocate for healthy living and sits on the board of the Native Wellness Institute, a nonprofit that creates wellness programs for communities across the United States. He lives and breathes his dedication to an ancestral diet and exemplifies a clean lifestyle full of fitness and exercise.

"Eating ancestral foods is simply a return to a holistic lifestyle," Collins says. *"It is restoring our collective spiritual connection to growing, hunting, and harvesting our own food to reestablish optimum health of individuals, families, communities, villages, and nations. The readoption of ancestral foods should be a permanent shift to be passed down for future generations to enjoy."*

Chantal Rondeau is the blogger behind Life and Times of a Modern Day NDN Princess. She lives in Vancouver.

Anthony "Thosh" Collins is a Pima photographer based in Phoenix. He studied at San Francisco Art Institute and travels all over North America for his photography business Thoshography.

Ceremony in the City

Tasha Spillett

Nehiyaw iskwew niya—I'm a Cree woman, from Treaty 5 and Treaty 6 on my maternal line, and on my paternal line my family is from the island of Trinidad. I'm from the Spirit Bear Clan, and I was born and raised in Winnipeg, Manitoba, which is known as the largest unofficial urban rez in Canada. If you've ever visited my home, you know what I'm talking about, and if you haven't, astum oma—come here and see for yourself!

I ceremony because it nurtures my spirit, it reminds me of where I come from, and it helps me to be strong enough to do the work that I do. I love the feeling of being surrounded by my relatives, laughing, teasing, sharing stories—I even love the tears that sometimes flow. I love letting my voice dance to the beat of Uncle's drums and the way my skin and hair smell like medicine after. Attending ceremony helps me put the pieces of myself together.

Every day, in the core of the city, in a neighborhood known for its violence, my students and I begin our learning day with a smudge. We light our medicine, and we cleanse ourselves. Sometimes people think that ceremony belongs only in certain places. I like to think of life as ceremony, so wherever life is happening is where ceremony belongs. I also think it's important for Indigenous people living in urban areas to reclaim spaces to honor their spiritual being. I've put offerings out in public parks in the city, and I've laid tobacco down by trees in the middle of downtown. We are given ceremony to help us navigate our lives; we carry it with us wherever we go. Even in the middle of a concrete jungle, it still pulses in our veins.

Ceremony isn't always a lodge or a certain item, nor is it locked in a certain period of time. It's how we choose to lead our lives and conduct ourselves. We can live traditionally and still make use of modern technology. Our ancestors were brilliant and innovative—that's how they were able to survive. I think they would want us to take full advantage of all that's available to us to strengthen ourselves and our communities and to care for our homelands.

Tasha Spillett is a high school teacher in Winnipeg, Manitoba, and is pursuing her master's degree in Land-based Indigenous Education at the University of Saskatchewan. Spillett is a ceremony woman, a sundancer, and a ceremony and powwow singer.

Mohawk

Manhattan in

K awennáhere Devery Jacobs (Mohawk) thought acting was an unrealistic career choice. At 20, she was completing a youth and cultural intervention program at John Abbot College in Montreal and working as a residential support worker at a Native women's shelter when she landed the role of Aila in *Rhymes for Young Ghouls*. The film went on to win Best Canadian Feature Film at the 2013 Vancouver International Film Festival, and Jacobs was nominated for Best Performance by an Actress by the Canadian Screen Awards. And the opportunities started to come. She was signed by Circle of Confusion, a New York– and Los Angeles–based management team. Jacobs left her home on the Kahnawake Reserve to move to New York City to pursue her acting career.

What's life like in New York? Did you face stereotypes?

I haven't faced Native stereotypes as much as I've faced ignorance. Most people think I am either Hispanic, or Filipino, or some form of ethnic mix. When I mentioned my race, I'd typically be met with a "Really? But you don't look Native American! What percentage are you?" Ugh. That's everywhere though, I guess.

How do you stay connected to culture in New York City?

Apparently New York has the highest population of Indigenous people of any city in the United States. I wouldn't have thought that had I not heard the statistic. To keep connected to the culture, I found time to attend cultural teach-ins such as Genocide Denial in North American Culture and the Two-Row Wampum Renewal Campaign. I spent time with Mohawk ironworkers from home who are building skyscrapers in Manhattan. Oh, and I also traveled back home a lot!

Why did you decide to leave New York?

I moved to New York City to get my foot in the door of the American film industry and to go on more in-person auditions. However, what ended up happening was that 90 percent of my auditions were self-tapes that were sent to Los Angeles and different cities. I was paying so much more money to live in NYC only to do self-taped auditions that could be recorded from anywhere in the world. New York can be lonely. There are millions of people, but it can be extremely cold. It didn't make sense to be away from my family, friends, boyfriend, and community when I could record my auditions from home.

I live in Montreal full-time now and bus it to New York and stay with friends whenever I need to audition in person or meet with directors. I really, really like NYC and would live there again, just not completely by myself, not for the film industry, and especially not to save money.

"New York has the highest population of Indigenous people of any city in the United States. I wouldn't have thought that had I not heard the statistic."

Actress Kawennáhere Devery Jacobs lives in Montreal. She is writing and directing a short film, *Stolen*.

NEW YORK

Traditional Territory - Lenape

"It's funny—in some ways, I'll feel so far away from my culture living in New York, and in other ways, closer. I may not be able to find a decent piece of fry bread, but I can still participate in my own way. My apartment is covered in beaver fur pillows and dream catchers that my aunt made, which gives me a little taste of home. But chic. People think my stuff is from, like, Crate and Barrel."

— Christain Allaire
(Ojibway, Nipissing First Nation), writer

> " I love that I can walk down the street and see familiar friendly neighbors and family members. It really is a community within a community. "

COMMUNITY
WITHIN A
COMMUNITY

Charlene Johnny-Wadsworth (Quw'utsun' Tribes, S'amuna') lives on the Squamish Nation, Capilano Reserve in Vancouver. It's one of three urban reserves in Vancouver and one of more than 120 urban reserves across Canada.

"According to my non-Native friends, "I am 'lucky' to live on the Squamish Nation, Capilano Reserve. It is the divide of West and North Vancouver, and it is close to the downtown area."

"" I have lived in downtown Vancouver and on the North Shore, but I prefer to live on the reserve. I'm in the city almost every day for work; it's busy and it's full of people. It's much more serene at Capilano. I wake up to birds chirping and occasionally the smell of smoked salmon wafting over from my neighbor's smokehouse. "

> **"** I hang out in Gastown quite often. It's one of the best locations in the city to photograph. Check out Hill's Native Art Gallery. Of all the touristy shops in Gastown, it is one of the few that carries authentic Native art — and my art is there. **"**

Charlene Johnny-Wadsworth is a photographer and a production and marketing manager at Native American Apparel.

Long-Distance Rez Romance

Breanna Doucette-Garr

My boyfriend and I officially met through Facebook. We had seen each other in person before but had never spoken a word. We knew of each other because of our love for volleyball. We had gone to the North American Indigenous Games together, both of us playing for the Saskatchewan volleyball team. But still we never spoke to each other. After I saw him once again at another tournament, I got up the courage to add him on Facebook. LOL. Anyway, he obviously admired me as much as I did him because he messaged me. One thing led to another, and we became infatuated with each other. The only problem was he lived four hours away on the Makwa Sahgaiehcan First Nation, and I lived in Saskatoon, where I was born and raised. Being that we were only 17 (going on 18), we didn't get many opportunities to see each other, especially since I was working all summer. Whenever I had time, I would hop on a bus and endure the five-hour bus ride to go see him. He made many attempts to come see me as well. After five years, one kid, and about ten breakups and makeups later, we are still together and plan on getting hitched! Of course, not for a while! Or not until I am done university, which is about another five years. We are still very young! We live in a small basement suite in Saskatoon with our daughter. It's not much but that's not what matters. What matters is we love each other very much and have gotten this far.

Breanna Doucette-Garr (Dene, English River First Nation) is a student at University of Saskatchewan.

SHATTERING STEREOTYPES

Through activism and the arts, young Natives
challenge and overcome the racism and
discrimination they face in urban environments.

Perception

Photo series by Winnipeg artist K.C. Adams (Oji-Cree)

In one photo, the models share racist remarks they
have experienced. In the other, they label themselves.

FETAL ALCOHOL SYNDROME?

Look Again...

NUNGOHS (Ojibway/Potawatomi)

A daughter, niece, straight 'A' student, YouTuber, violinist, track star and wants to be a veterinarian.

HOOKER?

LOOK AGAIN...

APRIL SINCLAIR (OJIBWAY)

A mother, daughter, girlfriend, sister, high school graduate, working mom, loves apples and coffee and is social assistance free!

DRUG DEALER?

Look Again...

JAMES LATHLIN (CREE)
A father, son, youth counselor, motivational speaker, coach, author, rapper and an aspiring stand up comedian.

SQUAW?

Look Again...

KC ADAMS (OJI-CREE)
A wife, mother, twin, artist, educator, homeowner, tax payer, curler, who paid for university herself.

"There are so many Indigenous people in Winnipeg who are leaders in their community and living normal or average lives. However, their stories never make it into the newspapers or on social media. This photo series is an attempt to combat the stereotypes of First Nation, Inuit, and Métis people."

– K.C. Adams

K.C. Adams is a multidisciplinary artist whose work ranges from photography and ceramics to sculpture and kinetic art.

Kill
the Indi

" You're coming to a city where you're not even welcome.
You're made to feel shame."

READING, WRITING, AND RACISM

Neebin Ishkoday (Oji-Cree) on how moving to the
city to attend high school ignited her activism

When I was 14 years old, I moved to Thunder Bay from my reserve to go to high school. We don't have a high school on my reserve. It's a small isolated fly-in community in the far north of Ontario.

Moving to the city was a huge culture shock. There are only a few hundred people in the community I grew up in. Everyone is like family. I went from a class of ten of us into a non–First Nations school with close to a 1,000 students. I went to a public school instead of Dennis Franklin Cromarty, where kids from reserves usually go (see sidebar).

I was lucky. My family moved with me. A lot of kids came up to Thunder Bay by themselves, so they didn't have any family support. They moved into boarding homes where they didn't know the people. The boarding homes had a lot of issues. My friends told stories about the fridge being locked up, of not being allowed to go into the living room. Some of the houses were drug houses where people only take in students for the money they receive monthly. I find it to be sort of like residential school– youth being forced to move out of their communities into an urban setting, having to leave their homes. That's exactly what residential school was.

In high school, I had to learn a whole new way of living and interacting. Where I come from, our cultural interactions are different. The way we interact with each other is more reserved. You don't look people in the eyes as a sign of respect. You hold back a bit as a sign of respect. In Thunder Bay, it was the opposite. People were loud and in each other's faces, very expressive. It took me a long time to get used to. It took me years to look someone in the eye.

At first, I kept so much to myself. I was very timid. Thunder Bay is a very hard place to live in. It's infamous for its racism and discrimination. Walking down the street, Native youth have things thrown at them from moving cars. A few

Dennis Franklin Cromarty School

·

Since 2000, eight teenaged Aboriginal students have died while away from their remote reserves attending high school in Thunder Bay. Of the eight, seven attended Dennis Franklin Cromarty School, a high school for Aboriginal students. The other was a student at Matawa Learning Centre, an alternative high school program for Aboriginal students.

·

Daniel Randall Levac was stabbed to death outside a movie theater in October 2014. The other teens—Jordan Wabasse, Kyle Morriseau, Reggie Bushie, Robyn Harper, Paul Panacheese, Curran Strang, and Jethro Anderson—died under suspicious circumstances. Families want to know whether the deaths were suicides that could have been prevented or whether they were homicides. An inquiry into their deaths was called in 2012, but it has been delayed.

·

These Aboriginal students attended federally funded high schools that receive roughly half the funding per student that a traditional Ontario public high school receives. Dennis Franklin Cromarty School has found funding and tried to implement better support mechanisms for teenage students attending from distant communities.

·

years ago, someone spray-painted "Kill the Indians" on a billboard. At the mall, you're followed in the stores by security. Especially in 2013, when Idle No More was starting, it was really bad. I was scared to walk down the street. There was a group of men who were taking First Nations women off the street and out of town and assaulting them. They said to the women, "We're targeting you because we don't believe you should have treaty rights." It roused me up to talk about it.

I had run-ins with teachers who spoke out against First Nations rights and issues in the classroom. I had to report a teacher for that reason. He said a lot of things that attacked my identity. At the time, I couldn't even speak up for myself. I didn't know how to explain myself. My non-Native classmates didn't understand me at all. In my grade 10 history class, we had one week of learning about residential schools. I was the only Native person in the class. A non-Native boy beside me was pointing and laughing at this old woman in a film who was telling about her residential school life. She was crying, and all he could do was laugh. It's hard because when you're 13 or 14 years old, you don't know who you are. You're coming to a city where you're not even welcome. You're made to feel shame. Until I moved away from my community, I thought suicide was normal. I thought drug abuse was normal. That was what I knew. All of my grandparents were in residential school. And my mom attended residential school. But they didn't talk about it or its effects on them and our lives. In Thunder Bay, I started questioning how I saw myself, and how I saw my culture, and how I fit in to not just my community and among my friends and family but in to larger mainstream society like Thunder Bay, and even how I fit in to Canada as a whole. That's why I'm so passionate about advocacy and learning and teaching about the issues. We need to learn how to speak up for ourselves—especially young people who face racism and discrimination.

Neebin Ishkoday now works with an advocacy group supporting First Nations students in achieving their educational goals.

Kill the Indians

"I was scared to walk down the street."

Stealing Health

Poem by Jessica Metcalfe (Turtle Mountain Chippewa)

Her radiation drains me,
stealing my health.
On Fridays, I can feel
her bad glow
penetrating
my stale blue office walls.
Sage explodes in this room.
She wrote about Navajo witchcraft—
the only researcher to do so.
She was warned about Indian power.
Her research lab of sand and color
swirl out of control,
as organs fail and limbs shatter.
Large white pills
mixed with foolish attempts
of misused power
break down in her bowel.
I spend fewer hours in her office,
protecting my own health
from her desperate grasp.

Jessica Metcalfe holds a PhD in American Indian Studies from the University of Arizona and writes about Native American art, fashion, and design. She also owns and operates the Beyond Buckskin Boutique, which sells Native American fashion.

WINNIPEG

**Traditional Territory - Anishinaabeg, Cree,
Oji-Cree, Dakota, and Dene peoples,
and the homeland of the Métis Nation**

"Winnipeg has garnered a lot of attention
on the grounds that we are 'the most racist
city in Canada.' Have I experienced racism
for myself? Of course. I've been called every
stereotype in the book: 'drunken Indian,'
'welfare mooch.' Does that mean that my city
is the most racist? Well, it isn't from where I
stand. Growing up in the city, I've seen the rich
diversity that Winnipeg has to offer and have
made many great friends from all walks of life.
I love my city and the people in it. I do feel that
we still need to learn to come together more.
Not as an Indigenous community but as the
community of Winnipeg on Treaty 1 land."

*– Maggie Moose
(Cree, Nelson House First Nation),
writer, filmmaker, and musician*

This young duo Mob Bounce are now known as "conscious" hip-hop heads, but back in the day, they used to be heavily influenced by gangster rap. MCs Heebz the Earthchild (Travis Hebert–Cree/Métis) and Craigy Craig a.k.a. the Northwest Kid (Craig Edes–Gitxsan Nation) are now spitting rhymes with a strong narrative of resistance.

MOB BOUNCE

RED RAGE

Can you tell me about the progression of your lyrics from when you started Mob Bounce three years ago?
When we started, we were living in the city. (Travis was doing a Native studies program at the University of Alberta in Edmonton and Craig attended the Capilano University in Vancouver.) We were immersed in the urban Native populace and met a lot of socially conscious people. Post-secondary education introduced us to so much history and current Indigenous affairs that it left us both in a state of red rage.

At the time, we didn't understand how our youth experiences affected us. We wrote songs that glorified psychedelics, partying, and smoking weed. Then we started experimenting with traditional drum on a track and it opened us up to expressing our cultural identity.

What has changed for you both since that time?
We woke up. After finishing and reflecting on our mixtape, we were able to identify what old patterns no longer served us. We realized that it wasn't what was going on in the world but what was going on within. We became aware of our healing journey and started that path. It was the ultimate paradigm shift.

Do you feel you have a responsibility to Indigenous youth?
Absolutely. We all have a responsibility to the youth, Indigenous or not. We grew up in the intergenerational effects of colonization. There was lots of alcohol and dysfunctional behaviors around us. We learned how to self-regulate and apply our creativity to our healing journey. The youth are the future, and the continuation of our entire existence depends on making those connections between our youth and our ancestral wisdom.

Where does that sense of responsibility come from?
Our responsibility is giving the youth as much as we are capable of. We have developed skills that allow us to live our potential. We want the youth to obtain those skills at a younger age than we did, so that they can achieve a sense of wellness. Culture has been stuck and unable to move forward and adapt. We have experienced the disconnection youth have with their cultural identity due to colonization. Our music is modern-day culture and we embed teachings and values that are purely Indigenous. Youth need something that is accessible that resonates with them.

What type of work do you both do with Indigenous youth?
The harshest realities that we see in our communities are depression, suicide, alcoholism, and substance abuse. One of the main goals is to educate the youth around oppression and cultural conditioning. We do this through different forms, whether it be art, music, spirituality, culture, or Native studies/social studies.

Your lyrics speak to a number of heavy issues such as suicide, intergenerational trauma, poverty, and loss of culture—do you feel the need to capture this struggle?
We never meant to, but we know now our generation must speak out against all the injustices that have executed this struggle. It's been prophesied that we are the generation that will make the necessary changes to ensure a better world for our future generations.

Indigenous youth can be affected by intergenerational trauma, which could leave them in a state of distress, or what Craig has called "a state of midnight." Can you expand on this?
It's all nature and nurture. Nature being our genetics, and nurture being our epigenetics. We pick up things in this world that don't belong to us; I'm speaking of energy in the felt sense. We can hold things for other people, and not necessarily see that we're hurting ourselves, or enabling someone else. It all comes down to epigenetics and how colonization affected our framework, and how we pass that onto the future generations. Being in the state of midnight is living in perpetual worry about whatever it is we're secretly carrying.

What Is Epigenetics?

Epigenetics is the study of the molecular changes to our genes caused by stress and trauma. These changes negatively impact health and well-being and can be inherited.

"When we started Mob Bounce we were living in the city. Post secondary education introduced us to so much history and current Indigenous affairs that it left us both in a state of red rage."

— Mob Bounce

LOVE YOU
SOME INDIANS

SPOKEN WORD BY ROANNA SHEBALA (DINE)

Everyone in Cleveland loves the Indians!
Everyone loves them some Indians!
Love you some Indians.
Be The Indian.
Not The Cowboy.
Throw on a war bonnet
Tell me it's fashion
Tell me how imitation is the sincerest form of flattery.

Go to your local truck stop.
Buy some dream catchers made from China.
Hang them on your rearview mirror of
Your Jeep Grand Cherokees,
Your Pontiacs,
Your Winnebagos
As you drive down I-40 your vehicles catch the dreams
Road killed by Manifest Destiny
The whole time the radio chimes:
This land is your land, This land is my land . . .

Love you some Indians
Honor them by making them mascots.
Turn them into cartoon characters.

Costume yourselves in crimson paint.
Use blood from Redskins.
Smear it all over.
Cover every inch.

Add big black eyes.
Big smile.
White, white teeth.

Don't forget fake feathers.
Cover your skin,
Don't tell me it doesn't come with privilege
Cover it,

Hide like you are ashamed of pigment.
Like it separated you from
the norm.

Tan that hide
Work beneath suns.
Turn that skin so scarlet it becomes purple in the shade.

Add feathers.
Add bows and arrows.
You are Indian.

Dance.
This stadium is your bonfire.
You are Indian.

Practice your tomahawk chop.
You are Indian.

Cheer for the Braves.
That have a higher enlisting rate in our armed forces.

Cheer for the Kansas City Chiefs
As they take the field for the halftime spectacular

Welcome the Seminoles
As the ghost of Osceola
Haunts the end field.

Washington Redskins.
Don't change your name
Instead hashtag Redskins Pride
Make social media our battleground.
We all know that Indians don't have Twitter accounts.
We still use smoke signals.

Applaud the Cleveland Indians'
Chief Wahoo's bright white choppers
Casting reflections
On how to
Love you some Indians.

Go paint the town!
Double coat over history.
Whitewash the red bricks of the reservations.
Let's have Indian Day at our schools
Use November to teach students
the Turkey dance with color construction paper headdresses and tepees.

Now, go home
Wash off the paint.
Go back.
Back to your thinking.
You honored your team.
Back to thinking you honored
The Indian.
We are only costumes,
Back to thinking
We only come out at halftime
Back to thinking you will only find us in westerns and Disney films.
Back to thinking,
That we only exist in history books.

Go back to thinking
It's all just fun and games.
Now, shake my hand.
Ignore how your fingers lasso around my wrist
Tying each of us to our ancestors.
Yet we still survive.
Now, tell me how knowing me is your privilege,
And how you love you an Indian.

Marvin Andrews Way

PHOENIX

**Traditional Territory - Akimel O'odham (Pima)
and Xalychidom Piipaassh (Maricopa) Tribes**

"Indigenous life, it's not hard. But it's not easy.
People have these stereotypes of you and you
have to convince them otherwise. Phoenix
is great because there are a lot of Natives
here. So there's a big community and lots of
programs and gatherings where you can talk
to people. There are also a lot of other people
here who aren't Native and don't know about
Natives. They say things like 'You live in the
city? I thought you lived on a reservation. You
have a house? I thought you lived in a teepee.'
It's hard to convince people—adults especially.
They think we don't exist anymore."

*— Talon Long
(Sicangu Lakota, Diné), grade 8 student*

The American Dream Is Alie and Well

artistic
Freedom

Multidisciplinary conceptual artist Nicholas Galanin (Tlingit/Unangax̂) is redefining "Native art" for the modern world. His work challenges the appropriation of Native culture and depiction of Indigenous peoples in popular culture.

From a long line of Northwest Coast artists, Galanin has lived, studied, and created in Sitka and Juneau, Alaska; London, England; and New Zealand, Montreal, and Seattle.

"In the North American art world, I experience racism and stereotyping everywhere. Often. It's not always an active 'Oh, you can't come here.' It's a more subtle institutionalized version of it.… They see my work based on my ethnicity as 'Native American art' belonging in a natural history museum with dinosaur bones."

Inert

Metatheory

"Our communities change, our relationships to the land change, our local knowledge of the land also adopts and grows in urban space. We are influenced by and are part of a beautiful diversity in these urban communities. Our relationship with the land and environment is real and sincere. Traditional art is always moving and engaged with our relationships to land, environment, and society. This will move as our relationships do."

BUILDING BRIDGES

In pursuing academic, professional, and political goals, Native youth strengthen their communities and build relationships with non-Natives, teaching them about Native culture to the benefit of all.

City Girls

Maggie and Michaela (Cree/Dene) are cousins and best friends. Maggie, 15, was born and raised in Saskatoon. Michaela, 17, moved to Saskatoon two years ago. She was born in Meadow Lake, a small city in northern Saskatchewan, and lived there and in Beauval, on the English River First Nation, the girls' home reserve.

Photographs by Tenille Campbell (Dene, English River First Nation, Métis) of Sweetmoon Photography

"We've always spent time together as a family on the rez, praying, at sweats and big family gatherings."

"We stay connected to Native culture by praying a lot, spending a lot of time as a family, and going to an Indigenous church."

"The schools are really good in the city."

"We hang out with both Native and non-Native kids."

"We learn about Indigenous culture in classes, but our non-Native classmates probably don't know as much as they could."

"In the city, you don't get to look at the stars like you can on the rez ...

... In Beauval, you can go outside and see hundreds of stars."

What It Means to Be an Aboriginal Student Today

Stephanie Willsey (Ojibwe/Chippewa) on her modern Indigenous identity

I am a First Nations Canadian, of the Chippewa, or Ojibwe, community of Rama, Ontario. I was raised off the reserve but only a short drive away, and I am there often.

Being Native is often characterized by deprivation and suffering—be it with respect to land, language, or identity—and, unfortunately, this is often the truth. My grandmother was forced to reject her Native language, culture, and customs as a child through a tragically misguided view that she, like all other Aboriginal people, would be better served by assimilating into the "white" world. The fabric of family life was shredded within

"I am not white. I simply have a modern Indigenous identity."

Aboriginal communities for generations, and many of the issues that exist today in these communities are a result of this governmental policy.

However, Aboriginal students in college and university today were born in a much more tolerant time. I live in a more socially inclusive and progressive era. In a liberal and diverse a city as Montreal now is, my college experiences have been inclusive. Being an "Aboriginal student" today means something very different from what it did even a couple of decades ago.

I am well integrated, perhaps seemingly "assimilated" with fellow students at my university. That being said, I am not white. I simply have a modern Indigenous identity. Just because I have not been directly affected by the suffering of previous generations does not make me any more or less Indigenous than any other.

Being Aboriginal is so much more than being a victim. It was an entire culture before the settlers arrived. And despite its low profile in urban Canadian society and in the media, it remains so. There is so much more that defines us, even off the reserve. I always have been very much a part of the First Nations community. Our culture is reliant on kin connections, and the Grandfather Teachings, which are moral teachings that have been passed down in my family; similar concepts of wisdom, love, respect, bravery, honesty, and so on can be found in many religions and cultures around the world. We really aren't that different.

I am among the very luckiest of our culture. I am very aware of that and do not for a second take that for granted. And I do not want to minimize the problems that remain. I know that not all legal issues have been

---

> "There is so much more
> that defines us,
> even off the reserve."

---

cleared regarding our people, land, and status. Yet, we have made tremendous progress, and I hope to be part of an even more successful future generation of Aboriginals. Now, more than ever, it is possible to hold on to and be proud of my Native heritage while also being part of a larger and more heterogeneous community.

Stephanie Willsey is a full-time student in philosophy, sociology, and political science at McGill University in Montreal.

CALGARY

Traditional Territory - Kainai Nation, Piikani Nation, Siksika Nation, Stoney Tribe, and Tsuu T'ina Nation

"Calgary has incredible mountains, land, sunsets. I want people to educate themselves about the land that they're on. It's important to know about who was here caring for the land before we were. That land is giving you water and support. I don't understand why people don't care. The land is important if you're Native or not. It's not a Native-person thing to care about the land."

— *Imajyn Cardinal*
(Cree, Dene), grade 11 student

Dear Native College Student,

You Are *Loved*

Dr. Adrienne Keene (Cherokee) wrote this post
on her blog after a Native student at Stanford,
her alma mater, committed suicide.

Dear Native College Student,

You are loved. You are loved so deeply and immensely that there are not words to convey the power of that love. Your ancestors love you. Your family loves you. Your friends, roommates, classmates love you. Your professors love you. Your RA (Resident Advisor) loves you. The student support staff and administrators love you. We love you. And we need you. We need you here, we need you to fight, and survive and thrive. But above all else, please, please know that you are loved.

Last week, a Native student at my alma mater, Stanford, took his own life. I didn't know this student personally. I didn't know his joy, his love, his pain, or his fear—but I know the campus community he was a part of and that he has left behind. I know how broken they feel, how devastated, and how empty. I know because we felt it, the exact same feelings, seven years ago when our classmate, friend, and little brother took his life.

I know, for you as a Native student, things are not easy. I know that it may feel like there are very few people on campus who understand you, understand where you come from, and the pressures you face above and beyond other students of color. Sometimes your fellow non-Native students don't and can't understand what it means to be you.

These are the things that keep me up at night. I worry endlessly about the personal costs of pushing you to college. In my research I focus on college access and transition for Native students. I talk about reframing Western education from a tool of colonialism to a tool of self-determination and liberation. I talk about nation-building and your responsibilities as a tribal citizen.

"We as Native people still only make up less than 1 percent of college students nationally, but that is still thousands of students, thousands of alumni who made it, who want to support you, and who love you."

I share stories of goodness and success to show you, your communities, and colleges that you can do it—because you can. But I worry constantly about the pressures and the costs to you. I worry that we're selling you a false bill of goods.

The students in my dissertation talked to me about the sacrifices they make in order to "give back" with their college degrees. One of my pre-med students schedules her days so tightly she has to include her times to sleep and eat, or she won't. Another gets up every day at 5 a.m. so he can greet the sun and pray, offering his corn pollen on the edge of his dorm next to a dumpster so he can face his sacred mountain. I think about my Native friends and how many of us have struggled with depression, anxiety, and suicidal thoughts while in college.

Because we are not just in college for ourselves. We are there for our communities and our people, and there is an expectation that we will use our degree to help make change. But this is an enormous pressure. Especially when the paths to giving back aren't clear and instead are paved with resistance from our own communities,

> "... many of us have struggled with depression, anxiety, and suicidal thoughts while in college."

accusations of "thinking we're better" than those back home, and tribal governments who won't even look at résumés from their young educated citizens. Our classmates don't have to weigh these pressures daily.

Take the time to tell your friends and fellow classmates how much they mean to you—thank them for the late nights of easy mac and laughter, for the study sessions, for the evenings of smoky fry bread kitchens, and for listening. The only way to counter the invisibility we often feel is to truly see others, and let them see us. Because college isn't just hard, it's also amazing and fun and bright. There is often more laughter than tears, and the relationships that form are so important to hold on to.

Asking for help is one of the hardest things to do. I know. But please know that there are always people who care, even when it feels like you are alone. We as Native people still only make up less than 1 percent of college students nationally, but that is still thousands of students, thousands of alumni who made it, who want to support you, and who love you.

With all my heart,

Adrienne

Dr. Adrienne Keene graduated with a BA from Stanford University and a PhD from the Harvard School of Education. She is a postdoctoral fellow at Brown University with a research focus on college access for Native students. Her blog nativeappropriations.com pushes back against stereotypes of Native peoples.

NATIVE NETWORKER

Gabrielle Scrimshaw (Dene) on how connecting with the Aboriginal professional community in Toronto brought her business success

Gabrielle Scrimshaw was faced with a decision she never thought she'd have to make: Harvard or Stanford? At age 26, she was accepted into the Harvard Business School and the Stanford Graduate School of Business, the top two business schools in the world. Statistically speaking, it shouldn't have happened. Only 1 to 2 percent of the 10,000 applicants get accepted to both. But Gabrielle has always defied the statistics.

As an Indigenous woman born in northern Canada and raised by a single father, the statistics said she was more likely to drop out of high school than finish it, four times more likely to be a victim of homicide than her non-Native female classmates, and eleven times more likely to be reported missing. In her community, she grew up witnessing the legacy of residential schools, surrounded by poverty, substance abuse, and suicide.

Gabrielle focused on her studies and got a scholarship to attend the University of Saskatchewan in Saskatoon. She worked hard and graduated in the top 5 percent of her class with a bachelor of commerce and marketing, the first person in her family to get a postsecondary education. In 2010, when she was invited to Toronto to work in finance and become an associate in RBC's Graduate Leadership Program, she leapt at the chance.

After a few months in finance, she started to feel like she was in over her head. "I was so scared," she says. "I didn't know if it was the right

> "Whether I'm meeting with an elder discussing spirituality or sitting at a board table on Bay Street, I'm the same person in those moments."

> "If you're the first in your family to go to university, and many Aboriginal people are, or you're the first in your family to get a job in a large organization or start your own business, there are support gaps."

decision. I was afraid that I would be disconnected from my family and lose my sense of community." So she started looking for a place where she could connect with other Aboriginals and find support to grow as a young professional. To her surprise, there was no organization in the Greater Toronto Area that fulfilled that mandate. So she decided to create one.

She pitched the idea to management consultant Richard Wiltshire, and they cofounded the not-for-profit. What started as a small and simple idea—a way to give First Nations, Métis, and Inuit professionals the chance to connect—has grown into the Aboriginal Professional Network of Canada (APAC), with more than 700 members across the country. The organization offers Aboriginal professionals a supportive community, networking opportunities, and programs to develop professional skills. APAC also hosts events where Aboriginal students get matched and networked with Aboriginal professionals.

"If you're the first in your family to go to university, and many Aboriginal people are, or you're the first in your family to get a job in a large organization or start your own business, there are support gaps," says Scrimshaw. "If APAC can make people's lives a little better in one small way or somehow remove a challenge, then why wouldn't we?"

Scrimshaw says her experience with APAC has taught her a lot about herself and the importance of Aboriginal leadership. "Whether I'm meeting with an elder discussing spirituality or sitting at a board table on Bay Street, I'm the same person in those moments," she says. "APAC is just one small piece of a larger puzzle of this shifting of tides for the Aboriginal community."

Scrimshaw was the first Aboriginal woman to speak at TEDxToronto, the largest TEDx event in Canada.

Gabrielle Scrimshaw is the co-founder and president of the Aboriginal Professional Association of Canada and is currently pursuing her MBA at the Stanford Graduate School of Business in California.

TORONTO

Traditional Territory - Mississaugas of the New Credit

"Toronto is a hub for Indigenous culture.
So much is thriving here with an Indigenous
mandate or presence. Unfortunately, we're also
visible in other not-so wonderful ways. The visible
minority, we're seen on the streets."

— Sarain Carson-Fox (Ojibwe),
actor, dancer, choreographer, and stylist

TELLING OUR STORIES

Michael Woestehoff (Navajo) on his life as a communications specialist in Washington, DC

On choosing Washington, DC

I had two reasons for moving to Washington, DC, when I was 23. First, there needed to be more tribal citizens telling our stories from our perspective and through our eyes. Public relations, visual communication, and marketing in Indian country was out of our hands, and I thought that we needed to be in those positions, so I searched out those jobs. The second reason why I wanted to be in Washington was because of the surprising presence of LGBT people. It wasn't shamed or hidden from public view. It wasn't in just one neighborhood. It was all over. That was unheard of on my reservation. LGBT people in Washington had professional leadership positions, high levels of education, and mission-driven ambition that wasn't confined to their sexuality. The men and women in DC were not confined by their identity but proudly fought for respect. I love that all identities pursue higher visibility in our nation's capital.

On religion

When I was a kid in Ganado, Arizona, my mother took me and my siblings to her church, an old single-wide trailer with old shag carpeting and folding chairs facing a Latter-day Saints elder. My father then became interested in our spirituality and took us to a Lutheran church, like the one he attended in his childhood. When I was in 7th grade, our parents took us out of public school and enrolled us in a Catholic school. There, we had weekly mass, along with religion classes complete with nuns as our teachers. In college, I found an evangelical Christian church.

Now with all these different denominations, and understanding their historical relationships to Native people and to the LGBT community,

it would be easy to think that hearing some of their sermons might push me away from their defined Higher Power. But I never felt that way. Ever. I feel that the Creator has always walked with me and provided much-needed guidance and reassurance in my life.

It was important to find a church in Washington that opened its doors to me and understood who I am completely. It took a while. But my church has been the most uplifting part of being in this city. Perhaps this church is a little bit like me, a black sheep: wanting to give those without a voice visibility, eager to instill change, and excited to tell a story about our tribal communities.

Michael Woestehoff (Navajo, Kin Yaa'aanii/ Towering House Clan, German, and Scandinavian) earned a masters in communications and public relations from Georgetown University. He lives and works in Washington, DC.

NATIVE RENAISSANCE

Committed to their culture and communities,
Native youth are leading Indigenous revitalization
across Turtle Island (North America).

Art and Activism in Indian Alley

I ndian Alley is the unofficial name given to a stretch of alley in the Skid Row area of downtown Los Angeles. In the 1950s and 1960s, many Native Americans moved there from reservations as far away as Oklahoma because of a government program that promised job training and a better life (see p. 108.). Families were promised temporary housing and help with finding a job. But there were few jobs. Many Natives had no option but to live in cheap hotels near the crime-ridden Skid Row area. They faced prejudice, poverty, and loss of culture. Some ended up homeless and developed alcohol and drug addictions.

In 1974, the United American Indian Involvement (UAII) was set up at 118 Winston Street as a safe place for homeless Natives to stay. The streets were very dangerous and many people died from beatings and overdoses. This area became known as Indian Alley.

Native and non-Native artists and activists came together to turn this once-bleak neighborhood into an outdoor gallery. More than a dozen murals now line the street.

What Was the Urban Relocation Program?

In the 1950s, the United States government started the Urban Relocation Program to encourage Native Americans to leave Indian reservations, move to cities, and assimilate into the general population. From the 1950s to the 1980s, as many as 750,000 Natives migrated to the cities. Many came to Los Angeles, making it the US city with the largest Native population during that period. People from over 100 federally recognized tribes lived there at that time.

WE ARE STILL HERE

#DearNativeYouth

Social media connects the Native community in cities, suburbs, and reservations across Turtle Island (North America). Twitter is a popular platform to engage in Native activism.

Brook Spotted Eagle, a PhD student in social anthropology at the University of Washington, ignited a fire with her hashtag #DearNativeYouth. Native rappers, DJs, writers, educators, fashion designers, lawyers, and businesspeople have tweeted messages of pride and inspiration to Native youth.

 ALIYAH JADE
@aliyahjade8

#DearNativeYouth: don't let others tell our story. You are a storyteller, a scholar and you have a duty to let your light shine.

. . .

 LAST STAND MIXTAPE
@LastStndMixtape

#DearNativeYouth: your voice, your art, and your community are your power and healing.

. . .

 ROBERT SNACHE
@spirithands

#DearNativeYouth do something you love. Others will find you.

. . .

A TRIBE CALLED RED
@atribecalledred

#DearNativeYouth: Your existence is crucial.
We appreciate and love you.

• • •

DON KELLY
@thedonkelly

#DearNativeYouth: You're growing in size &
strength everyday, a force to be reckoned with.
Keep using that for positivity & progress!

NATIVE LIFE
@_Native_Life

#DearNativeYouth: don't be swayed by what
mainstream media considers Natives are like.
Be you and not anyone else. Let your voice
be heard.

• • •

FRANK WALN
@FrankWaln

#DearNativeYouth: you deserve to be happy,
healthy and respected no matter who you are or
where you're from.

OFFENDEDNDN
@_RuthHopkins

#DearNativeYouth Speak your mind. The world
desperately needs your perspective. Write, draw,
make videos, sing...show them who we are.

• • •

ROMEO SAGANASH
@RomeoSaganash

#DearNativeYouth, Globalization is not a threat,
just an occasion to hang on to your roots, and
embrace the World.

• • •

SHELLEY ESSAUNCE
@shelleyshell4

#DearNativeYouth You Matter! To your family,
your community and your nation!

• • •

IN OUR WAY

Saffron Thomas (Squamish Nation)
on standing up to racism

Racism is still around, whether we like it or not. One night I brought my boyfriend, who's Native, to one of my non-Native friend's parties. He didn't know anyone besides me. I went to the bathroom, and when I came back, I could tell something had happened just by the look on his face. He insisted that nothing was wrong. But, later he told me that while I was gone, one Caucasian male saw him and said something rude and uncalled for. He used a derogatory word and then said, "What is *he* doing here?" I felt terrible because my boyfriend didn't know anyone else there and no one heard or did anything about it at the time. When I told one of my friends, she was shocked that it happened and said how unacceptable that was. She told her boyfriend, and they ended up kicking the guy out.

When I told my parents and others about what had happened to my boyfriend, their common response was that they "can't believe that's still going on today." As a nation, I feel we are starting to come together and reacting and responding to racism in our way. We are reaching the point now where we are heard. We no longer are kept quiet and in the dark.

Saffron Thomas is a fashion business and creative arts graduate, a model, stylist, and creative director. She lives on the Mission Indian Reserve in Vancouver.

VANCOUVER

Traditional Territory - Skwxwú7mesh (Squamish), Tsliel-Waututh, and Xwméthkwyiem (Musqueam) First Nations

"I came to Vancouver to gain skills and knowledge of the business world. My intention has always been to use the knowledge and skill to give back to the community that helped me get to where I am now. Vancouver has provided that happy medium of business opportunity while having nature and Indigenous culture visibly present. It is encouraging to see the growing number of young Native professionals. We can all push each other to achieve more together."

— Seth Armitage (Secwepmec from Cstelen), financial services manager

One
World

Scientist Skaruianewah Logan (Akwesasne Mohawk Nation) on building a Native network

I was at a spoken word event in New York City, and I met a Native guy. He said, "You look Native." And I said, "Yeah, I'm Native." From there we figured out we were actually connected online. We exchanged information and became really good friends.

He was very, very city. He loved being a city Native. I had this amazing job as a research assistant at Columbia University that I loved even though it was hard. I had this resource—another city Native who understood the balancing act of coming from two very different lifestyles. Because a lot of the city Natives I met until that point weren't very traditional. He said, "No man. You've got to include the traditional thought. You have to make it one world. You can't separate them. Make this one experience. It's yours."

He was a great influence. I kept in contact with him over the years. He did a lot of traveling as a photographer. Through him I met other people. Once I had this great network of Native friends in different cities like Los Angeles or Chicago or Detroit, I realized I wasn't alone.

Skaruianewah Logan lives on the Onondaga Nation Reserve in New York State and is an associate scientist at Bristol-Meyers Squibb. She holds a masters of science in molecular and cellular biology from Brandeis University.

SpeakingUp

Musician iskwé (Cree/Dene, Irish) on why she
raised her voice on the issue of Canada's Missing
and Murdered Indigenous Women

It's important to be strong and stand up and say something. There's a lot of Indigenous women in the arts and entertainment who are very vocal. The song "Nobody Knows" (see lyrics on p. 120) is inspired by my endless frustration surrounding the lack of knowledge and understanding on the issue of Canada's Missing and Murdered Indigenous Women. I found myself explaining time and time again about just how bad the situation is, and got to a point where I needed to scream it out! Ha, so I screamed it out in a song.

As a kid growing up in Winnipeg, my parents did a good job of letting me be a kid without adding the stresses of life on me, but once I was nearing my teens, they prepped me for what life would be like as a young female in that city and in the world. The threat of sexual violence is unfortunately a reality for women, regardless of where they live. We are forever being trained in how to "keep ourselves safe."

In Cree, iskwé (pronounced iss-KWAY) means woman. I've been feeling quite silenced lately. For the album photo shoot, I beaded the word "iskwé" onto a band, and I put that word in front of my mouth. If we think of the murdered and missing women, they don't have the ability to say anything anymore. That was taken from them because they were Indigenous women. This is my reflection in my art, the way my spirit felt the need to speak up.

Nobody Knows

Lay me down now
lay me to the ground
lay me down now
lay me down in the shade

I won't be afraid, no I won't
I won't be afraid, no I won't
I won't be afraid
lay me down in the shade

Nobody knows, nobody knows
where we've been or where we go
nobody knows, nobody knows
where we've been or where we go
Nobody knows

I won't let you look away
I won't let you look away
I won't let you look away anymore

Lyrics by iskwé

Missing and Murdered Indigenous Women

More than 1,000 First Nations, Inuit, and Métis women and girls have been murdered between 1980 and 2012 in Canada, a murder rate more than 4.5 times higher than that of all other women in Canada. In addition, more than 100 Indigenous women and girls remain missing under suspicious circumstances. Aboriginal women are also nearly 3 times more likely than non-Aboriginal women to be victims of violent crime.

Faceless Doll Project: "Each statistic tells a story"
Students at the Eric Hamber Secondary School in Vancouver created these dolls and posters as part of the project to raise awareness about missing and murdered Indigenous women. *(Learn more on p.133)*

"My father was an amazing inspiration for pushing outside of the boundaries and reaching beyond the limits. Whether it was politics, activism, or acting, he was giving hope and proving that anything is possible because he was one of us, and he was doing amazing, seemingly impossible, things and making them a reality."

Tatanka with his father, Russell Means.

NDN
INNOVATOR

Tatanka Means (Oglala Lakota/ Omaha/Navajo) is a Hollywood actor, an award-winning comedian, a motivational speaker, and an entrepreneur with his own clothing line. He exemplifies the modern NDN millennials, individuals who defy convention and take on multiple roles to carve out careers that are creative and fulfilling. Tatanka is following in the footsteps of his father, Russell Means, who was a prominent member of the American Indian Movement and Native American activist, as well as a Hollywood actor.

"Indian people are always wearing multiple hats from work to home and family to our cultures and traditional ways. We incorporate our cultural backgrounds into everything we do."

"Managing these different roles can be tasking at times, but I like to be busy more than I like having downtime."

"I love spending time with my friends and relatives back home on the rez . It's where I grew up, where my roots are, but you can't stay home and hope someone hears about your talents and comes looking for you—you have to go and put forth the efforts to create opportunity for yourself and make your dreams a reality. I'm not saying it's impossible to make it happen from back home, but at some point you might want to be closer to wherever the work may be. Then we bring our talents home to help inspire our people."

Tatanka Means lives in Albuquerque with his family.

LOS ANGELES

Traditional Territory - Chumash Tribe, Tongva Nation, Tataviam Band

"The Indigenous culture is rich on this side of Turtle Island. Next to New York, we have the largest population of Indigenous peoples in the USA. With the film, music, TV, and movie industries as a main attraction, Hollywood has to be the capital of Indian Country!"

— *Crystle Lightning (Enoch Cree),*
film actress, MC with LightningCloud, DJ

*

EDGEWALKERS

Jessica Bolduc (Anishinaabe, Batchewana First Nation), the national youth representative for the Congress of Aboriginal Peoples' National Youth Council, on a new generation of Native leaders

I like to think of myself as an Edgewalker. Edgewalkers are a new generation of Aboriginal leaders who have no patience for the status quo, who are deeply interested in the potential of the future, and who have a hunger to contribute to a better world. We've learned from the past and are using our Indigenous world views and our understanding of modern systems to shape future possibilities that value the well-being of all rather than just the few.

Go out and find the Edgewalkers in your city. They are everywhere. Some you will find burning bright and blazing trails; where others, you'll have to look a little harder as they are at this moment, just sparks of light. They don't know it yet, but they are about to light their communities on fire.

*

Jarret Leaman (Ojibwe) from Concrete Indians series by Nadya Kwandibens (Ojibwe) of RedWorks Studio

Jessica Bolduc is the executive director of the 4Rs Youth Movement, working to build understanding among Indigenous and non-Indigenous youth, and is a board member of Community Foundations of Canada.

Urban Natives—

CANADA

1.4 million people identify as **Aboriginal**, i.e., **First Nations**, **Métis**, or **Inuit** in Canada

Total Canadian population: 33.5 million

Aboriginals *are* **4.3%** *of total Canadian population*

The Aboriginal population in Canada is growing more than 1.5 times faster than the non-Indigenous population.

From 1996 to 2011, the number of Aboriginals in urban areas grew 7%.

Urban Aboriginal children are more than 2 times as likely as non-Aboriginal children to live in poverty.

More Aboriginal women than men live in urban areas in Canada.

1.4 MILLION TOTAL ABORIGINALS

56% of Aboriginals live off reserve

44% of Aboriginals live on reserve

Cities with largest Aboriginal population

WINNIPEG, MANITOBA

EDMONTON, ALBERTA

VANCOUVER, BRITISH COLUMBIA

TORONTO, ONTARIO

CALGARY, ALBERTA

Sources:
Canada. Statistics Canada. Urban Aboriginal Peoples, Aboriginal Affairs and Northern Development Canada, Government of Canada, 2011 Census.
Fact Sheet. Urban Aboriginal Population in Canada, Aboriginal Affairs and Northern Development, Government of Canada. 2010-09-15

By the Numbers

UNITED STATES

5.2 million people identify as **Native Americans**, i.e., **American Indian** or **Alaska Native**

Total US population: 308.7 million

Native Americans are **1.7 %** of total US population

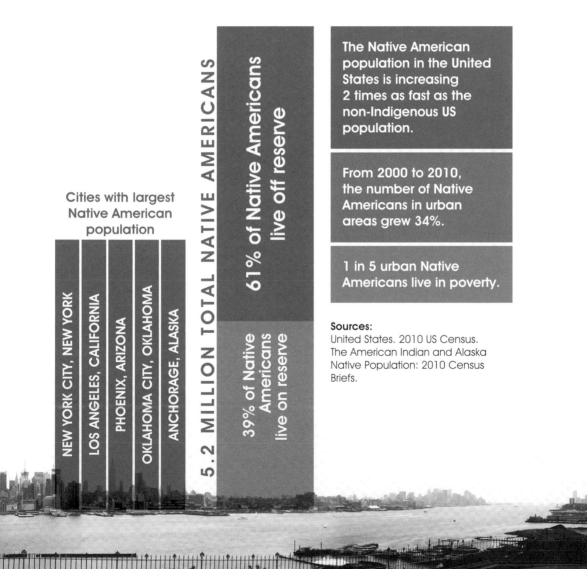

Cities with largest Native American population

NEW YORK CITY, NEW YORK

LOS ANGELES, CALIFORNIA

PHOENIX, ARIZONA

OKLAHOMA CITY, OKLAHOMA

ANCHORAGE, ALASKA

5.2 MILLION TOTAL NATIVE AMERICANS

61% of Native Americans live off reserve

39% of Native Americans live on reserve

The Native American population in the United States is increasing 2 times as fast as the non-Indigenous US population.

From 2000 to 2010, the number of Native Americans in urban areas grew 34%.

1 in 5 urban Native Americans live in poverty.

Sources:
United States. 2010 US Census. The American Indian and Alaska Native Population: 2010 Census Briefs.

Selected Bibliography

Amnesty International Canada. "Missing and murdered Indigenous women and girls: Understanding the numbers." *Human Rights* (blog). http://www.amnesty.ca/blog/missing-and-murdered-indigenous-women-and-girls-understanding-the-numbers.

Canada. Aboriginal Affairs and Northern Development Canada. Fact Sheet. *Urban Aboriginal population in Canada.* Last modified September 15, 2010. https://www.aadnc-aandc.gc.ca/eng/1100100014298/1100100014302.

Canada. Aboriginal Affairs and Northern Development Canada. *Urban Aboriginal Peoples.* Last modified December 1, 2014. https://www.aadnc-aandc.gc.ca/eng/1100100014265/1369225120949.

Center for Native American Youth. "Fast Facts on Native American Youth and Indian Country." Accessed May 26, 2015. http://cnay.org/uploads/FastFacts.pdf.

Environics Institute. "Urban Aboriginal Peoples Study", 2010. http://www.uaps.ca/wp-content/uploads/2010/02/UAPS_Summary_Final.pdf.

Lawrence, Bonita. *"Real" Indians and Others: Mixed-Blood Urban Native Peoples and Indigenous Nationhood.* Vancouver, BC: UBC Press, 2004.

Library of Congress. "Indian Removal Act: Primary Documents in American History." Last modified March 31, 2015. http://www.loc.gov/rr/program/bib/ourdocs/Indian.html.

Loppi, Samantha, Charlotte Reading, and Sarah de Leeuw. *Social Determinants of Health: Aboriginal Experiences with Racism and Its Impacts.* National Collaborating Centre for Aboriginal Health, 2014. http://www.nccah-ccnsa.ca/Publications/Lists/Publications/Attachments/131/2014_07_09_FS_2426_RacismPart2_ExperiencesImpacts_EN_Web.pdf.

National Urban Indian Family Coalition. "Urban Indian America: The Status of American Indian and Alaska Native Children and Families Today". A Report to the Annie E. Casey Foundation, 2007. http://caseygrants.org/wp-content/uploads/2012/04/NUIFC_Report2.pdf.

Newhouse, David, and Evelyn Peters, eds. *Not Strangers in These Parts: Urban Aboriginal Peoples.* Policy Research Initiative, Government of Canada, 2002. http://publications.gc.ca/collections/Collection/CP22-71-2003E.pdf.

PBS. "Assimilation, Relocation, Genocide: The Urban Relocation Program." *Indian Country Diaries.* September 2006. http://www.pbs.org/indiancountry/history/relocate.html.

Urban Aboriginal Task Force. Final Report. Commissioned by The Ontario Federation of Indian Friendship Centres, The Ontario Metis Aboriginal Association, and The Ontario Native Women's Association, December 2007. http://ofifc.org/sites/default/files/docs/UATFOntarioFinalReport.pdf.

Learn More

Read

King, Thomas. *The Inconvenient Indian: A Curious Account of Native People in North America*. Toronto: Penguin Random House Canada, 2012.

Kino-nda-niimi Collective, ed. *The Winter We Danced: Voices from the Past, the Future and the Idle No More Movement*. Winnipeg: Arbeiter Ring Publishing, 2014.

Saul, John Ralston. *The Comeback*. Toronto: Viking/Penguin Books, 2014.

Watch

CBC Newsworld. *Reds, Whites & the Blues*. Toronto, ON: CBC Learning, 2006.

Diamond, Neil, Jeremiah Hayes, and Catherine Bainbridge. *Reel Injun: On the trail of the Hollywood Indian*. Directed by Neil Diamond. Toronto, ON: Resolution Pictures and the National Film Board of Canada, 2009. Film, 86 min.

MacKenzie, Kent. *The Exiles*. Directed by Kent MacKenzie. New York, NY: Milestone Films, 1961. Film, 72 min.

Get Involved

Faceless Doll Project, Native Women's Association of Canada
http://www.nwac.ca/programs/faceless-dolls-project

VISIT OUR WEBSITE urbannativetribes.com

The Editors

Lisa Charleyboy is Tsilhqot'in from Tsi Del Del First Nation who lives in the unceded traditional territory of the Musqueam and Salish First Nations in Vancouver, BC. She is the cofounder and editor-in-chief of *Urban Native Magazine*, cocreator and host of Urban Native Girl TV, and co-editor of *Dreaming in Indian: Contemporary Native American Voices*. She has most recently found herself as a host of CBC Radio's New Fire and is finishing her EMBA in Aboriginal business and leadership program at Simon Fraser University. Visit her website at **lisacharleyboy.com**

Mary Beth Leatherdale is the writer and editor of many award-winning books and magazines for children and youth, including the critically acclaimed *Dreaming in Indian: Contemporary Native Americans Voices*. She consults on publishing and editorial projects and is the former editorial director at Owlkids. Visit her website at **www.marybethleatherdale.com.**

Acknowledgments

We're honored to have created this collection of stories, poetry, and artwork from such a talented, diverse group of young people. Thank you to the contributors for your honesty and generosity in sharing your experiences. A special thanks to Steven Paul Judd for allowing us to use his powerful artwork on the *Urban Tribes* cover and to Eyoalha Baker, Thosh Collins, and Nadya Kwandibens for their extra efforts in support of the project. Thanks to Savannah "Savvy" Simon for providing our closing quote.

We're also grateful to the many people who were interviewed or who submitted material whose words and pictures don't appear on the pages. Your insights were valuable and contributed to our deepening understanding of the issues. And to the academics and educators Dr. Bonita Lawrence, Elder Albert Marshall, and the late Dr. Gail Guthrie Valaskakis, thank you for your work and vision. It was a huge inspiration and guidance throughout the development process.

Thank you to the team at Annick Press for your belief in and patience with this sometimes unpredictable project. To Inti Amaratsu, our talented designer, thank you for turning our raw material into this beautiful, powerful book. And, last but certainly not least, to Joseph Boyden—huge thanks for your support of the project and your moving introduction. Sechanalyagh.

Contributors

K.C. Adams (Oji-Cree) • Christian Allaire (Ojibway) • Seth Armitage (Secwepmec) • Tyson Atleo (Nuu-chah-nulth) • Kristina BadHand (Sicangu Lakota/Cherokee) • Eyoalha Baker (Coast Salish/Squamish) • Jessica Bolduc (Anishinaabe) • Sarain Carson-Fox (Anishinaabe) • Maggie Campbell (Cree, Dene) • Tenille Campbell (Dene, Métis) • Imajyn Cardinal (Cree, Dene) • Thosh Collins (Pima) • Breanna Doucette-Garr (Dene) • Craig Edes (Gitxsan Nation) • Eric Hamber Secondary School, Vancouver • Nicolas Galanin (Tlingit, Aleut) • Travis Hebert (Cree, Métis) • iskwé (Cree/Dene, Irish) • Charlene Johnny-Wadsworth (Quw'utsun' Tribes, S'amuna') • Kawennáhere Devery Jacobs (Mohawk) • Steven Paul Judd (Kiowa/Choctaw) • Adrienne Keene (Cherokee) • Wab Kinew (Anishinaabe) • Nadya Kwandibens (Ojibwe) • Crystle Lightning (Hobbema/Cree) • Skaruianewah Logan (Akwesasne Mohawk Nation) • Talon Long (Sicangu Lakota, Diné) • Elder Albert Marshall (Mi'kmaq) • Michaela McIntryre (Cree, Dene) • Tatanka Means (Oglala Lakota/Omaha/Navajo) • Jessica Metcalfe (Turtle Mountain Chippewa) • Maggie Moose (Cree) • Pamela Peters (Navajo) • Chantal Rondeau (Hanjek Hudan Clan) • Gabrielle Scrimshaw (Dene) • Roanna Shebala (Diné) • Patrick Shannon (Haida) • Savannah "Savvy" Simon (Mi'kmaq) • Tasha Spillett (Cree) • Doug Thomas (Ojibway) • Saffron Thomas (Squamish) • Julaine Trudeau (Oji-Cree) • Matika Wilbur (Swinomish, Tulalip) • Stephanie Willsey (Ojibwe) • Michael Woestehoff (Navajo) • Stephen Zeigler

---

Credits

All photo collages created by Inti Amaterasu; p. 6 Photo by Inti Amaterasu; p. 16–19 Photos of Tyson Atleo by Eyoalha Baker; p. 20 Photo of Savvy Simon by Jordan Blackburn; p. 22–27 Food with Thought photos by Thosh Collins; p. 28–31 Photos of Tasha Spillett by Doug Thomas; p. 32 Photo of Devery Jacobs by Thosh Collins, p. 33 by Daniel Rowe; p. 36 Photo courtesy of Christain Allaire, background Inti Amaterasu; p. 38-41 Photos of Charlene Johnny-Wadsworth by Patrick Shannon; p. 42 Illustration by Kristina BadHand; p. 50–55 Illustrations by Kristina BadHand; p. 56 background by Inti Amaterasu; p. 58 Photo courtesy of Maggie Moose; p. 60–63 Photos courtesy of Mob Bounce; p. 64 Illustration by Kristina BadHand; p. 68 Photo courtesy of Talon Long; p. 78–83 Photos courtesy of Sweetmoon Photography/Tenille Campbell www.sweetmoonphotography.ca; p. 86-87 Photo courtesy of McGill University; p. 90 Photo of Adrienne Keene by Matika Wilbur from the Project 562 series www.matikawilbur.com; p. 94 Photo of Gabrielle Scrimshaw by CinemaWorks Photography – Jordan Presseault, p. 97 Celin Joseph; p. 98 Photo courtesy of Sarain Carson-Fox, background by Inti Amaterasu; p. 100 Photos courtesy of Michael Woestehoff; p. 104 Photo of Indian Alley by Stephen Zeigler; p. 106–107 Photos upper left and bottom right by Pamela Peters, all others by Stephen Zeigler; p. 108–109 Photos by Stephen Zeigler; p.110-111 Tweets illustrated by Kateryna Topol; p. 112 Photo of Saffron Thomas by Charlene Johnny-Wadsworth; p. 114 Photo courtesy of Seth Armitage; p. 116 Photo of Skaruianewah Logan by Richard Chase; p. 118-119 Photos of iskwé by Megan Wilson; p. 120-121 Photos and artwork courtesy of Eric Hamber Secondary; p. 122 Photo of Tatanka Means by Joshua Tousey, p. 123 "Braiding Hair" by Ilka Hartmann for the Omaha Tribal Historical Research Project; p. 124–125 Photos by Matika Wilbur; p. 126 Photo courtesy of Crystle Lightning; p. 129 Photo of Jarrett Leaman by Nadya Kwandibens/RedWorks Studio. Dreamstime.com images: p. 20 background, © Ramunas Bruzas; p. 58 background, © Gilles Deruyenaere; p. 68 background, © Chris Curtis; p. 84 background, © Fallsview; p. 114 background, © Vismax; p. 124 background, © Salvador Ceja.

"You can practice your culture anywhere. You can be Native anywhere; you don't have to grow up on a rez or grow up in a Native community to be Native. My generation has all this opportunity. So many warriors are coming together with positivity and love across Turtle Island (North America). There was a prophecy that a web would bring us all together and I believe that's the world wide web.

Social media is connecting us all closer now than ever. I have a lot of amazing Native brothers and sisters across Turtle Island who inspire me and motivate me. I really look up to a lot of Natives who are doing good things. A lot of people are fighting the good fight. So let's continue to make our ancestors proud."

— Savannah "Savvy" Simon (Mi'kmaq)